Rambling On

Ruth Y. Nott

Chiefland, FL, USA

To obtain copies of this book or obtain required permission
for use of material herein, email author:

ruth@ruthnott.com

ISBN 13: 978-0-9862792-4-9
ISBN 10: 0-9862792-4-2
Library of Congress Control Number: 2016931081

Published by Envision Books
Printed in the United States of America.

Preface

Time Flies

The older I get, the faster time flies
Yet words are slow to appear.
I've spent too much time on quilting,
Not enough on poems this year.
The days go by in a blur.
It's hard to pin my thoughts down.
They bump and tumble along
Taking root in infertile ground,
Trying to sprout and grow to a poem
But too often withering away
For lack of a nurturing hand
To keep them from going astray.
A few, though, have managed to thrive
And made their way to these pages
Crawling along on turtle feet
While time flies into life's next stages.

Table of Contents

Chapter 1 – Rambling On About God

Chapter 2 - Rambling On About Everyday Life

Chapter 3 - Rambling On About Quilting

Chapter 3 - Rambling on About Death

1

Rambling On About God

A Life in Peril

Somewhere there are children playing.
Somewhere the sun still shines.
Somewhere there's a life in peril.
It could be yours or mine.
Rockets flare and bombs explode
And bullets find their mark.
Extremists laugh and make heads roll
As evil lights the dark.
Somewhere God is watching
With tears upon His cheeks.
Somewhere angels hover
Too emotional to speak.
For all that God has given
In His creation of this earth
Lies in peril of destruction
Unless we realize its worth.
Somewhere there are children playing
But how long will that last
When we so carelessly destroy the earth.
I fear the die is cast.
Somewhere the sun still shines

As the battle plans unfold,
As terrorism takes its toll
On body, mind and soul.
Still somewhere God is watching
And in faith we hope and pray
For His loving intervention
Before the end of days.

Open Your Eyes to God

Somewhere out in the cosmos
The hand of God did wave
And all the stars and planets
Appeared and did behave,
Moving in perfect order
According to His plan
And then he looked upon the earth
And there created man.
He made the trees and animals
To benefit each other
To provide food and shelter
And protection one to another.
But somehow over the centuries
We lost track of the way He'd shown,
Forgetting the rules of God
While trying to make our own.
Now all of God's creation
Suffers from our mistake
Yet still He tries to woo us
Back into the fold
With new creations every day
For His children to behold.
When you awoke this morning

Did you see the golden dawn
And see the shadows of the night
Receding across the lawn?
Did you see the spider on his web
That sparkled with morning dew?
Or did you close your eyes again
And try to sleep anew.
We must open our eyes to God
To truly see His wonder.
And breathe again His healing breath
To break the spell we're under.
Open your eyes with each step you take
Truly look at His creation
Find the joy in newborn chicks
And geese in flight formation.
Touch a new formed ear of corn
And the dirt from which it feeds.
And know that God has put it there
To help supply our needs.
Have you seen the crimson sunset
Reflected on the clouds,
Watched the dolphins as they play
And said "Amen!" aloud?
We must open our eyes to God
And be thankful He still cares
We must help Him renew the earth again
Every day, every way, everywhere!

It's Almost Time for Christmas!

Sparkling lights and tinsel strings
And ornaments all around…
It's almost time for Christmas,
The day when Love came down
To a lowly Bethlehem stable.

Now joyful bells will ring
And carolers abound
It's almost time for Christmas,
Time to spread the love around
To whomever we are able.

With the star atop the tree
And snow upon the ground,
It's almost time for Christmas.
When the Christ-child can be found
In our hearts and in the manger on the table.

Did You...?

Did you get just what you wanted for Christmas?
Were your stockings filled with gifts galore?
Did Santa find his way down your chimney?
Could he possibly have brought you any more?

Did you take a moment out to just say "Thank you?"
Did you kneel and say a prayer for those in need?
Did you think about the children going hungry
And those denied the right to learn to read?

This world is so in need of intervention!
We need to pray and pray and pray and pray
That God will forgive our lack of caring
And show us how to change our lives His way.

Did you think He didn't care and give up hoping?
It's time to think again with hope renewed!
It's time to rally 'round our glorious Master,
Time to sound the battle cry and fill the pews!

Did you get just what you wanted for Christmas?
Shouldn't we be praying for even more...
Praying for more love and peace and mercy
As a brand new year comes knocking at our door?

The Christmas Gift

Sometimes we forget that God has a plan
That doesn't depend on the wishes of man.
Amy was told she could not conceive
By normal means, but she still believed.
Time after time in-vitro she tried
And time after time in failure she cried
A torrent of tears for the babies she lost
But she kept on trying no matter the cost.
When finally she managed to carry a child
For nine long months she must have smiled
As Tova Grace came into the world
And she was able to hold her first little girl.
Yes, sometimes we forget that God has a plan
That doesn't depend on the wishes of man.
As time went on, Amy would find
That God's blessings occur in His own good time.
For another child was growing now
A normal conception, and no one knows how
Except by God's will to bless them all.
The days sped by… and then they crawled.
In mid-December she reached the date
And passed it by… This child was late!
Then they planned to induce on Christmas Eve
But "there was no room in the inn" and she had to leave.
Then on Christmas day God said it was time…
"This child is on MY schedule, not on thine!
She's right on time. My gift is not late!
And now I give you my Reagan Kate.
I entrust her to you to love and raise
And to show her my love in so many ways."

Greater Than Any Gift

The toys are all made and packed in the sleigh
And Santa is waiting to be on his way!
The sleigh bells will jingle as he starts to take flight
While children lay sleepless all through the night.
What joy they will feel when the morning sun shines
As they run to see just what they can find.
Jolly old St. Nick is but Christmas icon.
But there was this babe with just straw to lie on.
The Son of God, of whom angels sing,
Is greater than any gift that Santa can bring!
So look to the top of that bright Christmas tree
And follow the star... He's waiting for thee!

The Better Gift

Santa Claus may watch to see
If we've been bad or good
And we may be on his gift list
If we've done the things we should.
But he cannot provide for us
The gift of eternal life
And he cannot protect us
Through our troubles and strife.
So wouldn't you surely rather be
Under our Father's watchful eye
And never have to wonder
If we'll join Him when we die?

Slipping Away

When we find ourselves slipping
And our faith not as strong,
We must turn back to the Lord
Before we do wrong;
Resolve to do better,
Spend more time in prayer,
Return to the pews
Where His word is shared.
This firm resolution
Carried out with zeal
Will straighten our paths
And our backsliding heal.

Invitation

Welcome to the party!
Come right on in!
A new year is beginning
As the old one ends.
Don't think of old problems
For those days are done.
Just think of the wonders
And blessings to come.
God has great plans
To brighten your days
And uplift your spirit
In His gentle way.
We celebrate a new year,
A new life, a new you.

Come meet your Host
And let Him prepare
The wine and the bread
Which He'd like to share.
Here you are family.
Here you can live…
Just open your heart
To all He can give!

Your Choice!

Did you know that salvation is free?
It doesn't cost one thin dime!
It's a choice you should make with glee
To live free with Jesus for all time
By simply confessing your belief in Him
And being dipped in the baptismal pool.
So take that step… Go out on a limb…
Ask forgiveness and ask Him to rule
Over all your life from now on.
Ask Him to show you the way of life
Which He led as the faithful Son
Bringing victory from torment and strife.
Did you know that salvation is free
And death is the cost of sin?
The choice is yours as He meant it to be
You can choose to lose… or to win!

Beautiful!

There is beauty in the Word
That shines like polished gold.
No matter what you've heard
Its wisdom will unfold
To enlighten every seeker.

There is beauty in each chapter,
In the lessons Jesus taught,
In the tears and in the laughter,
And the battles that were fought
At God's direction.

There is beauty in the birth
Of our Savior and our King
And His story that is worth
All the praise the angels sing
Yes, hallelujah!

There is beauty in each day
We are given by His love
And in His promise of the way
To join Him up above
In eternal peace.

Hallelujah for the beauty
In the holy name of Jesus!
Take up your cross and duty
And make His love the reason
For your thankful prayer.

I Am Thankful

For blessings received
When I am in need,
For friends to share
My joys and cares,
For love and grace
Since He died in my place.
It should have been me
Nailed to that tree.

That Time of Year

When spring arrives
And trees are budding green
And tiny yellow blossoms
On the lawn are seen,
It's time to think of planting,
Of digging in the soil,
Of dirty hands and broken nails
As tirelessly we toil
To bring the rainbow's colors
From the sky to earth below
In beds of beautiful flowers
We water and watch grow.
We pray for rain and sunlight
And prepare for bugs and drought;
And hope that God looks kindly
On our efforts to help Him out!

Then and Now

A long time ago
When I was just a kid
I knew little of religion
Or what various faiths did.

But the ritual of the Catholics,
The chants and songs,
Seemed so pleasing and familiar…
Almost like I belonged.

I used to imagine that
In another life and time
I had once been a nun
Devoted and kind.

But my life took a turn
As the years rolled by
And marriage and babies
Made me realize

That what may have been
In some other life
Is no comfort or cure
For this day's strife.

We must look for the answers
In the here and the now
With the help of Jesus
Not rituals and vows.

Lift Us Up

When this crazy world around us
Falls apart about our feet,
Stand by us Lord and lift us up!

Lift us up with gentle arms
Wipe away our futile tears
Heal our pain and mend our hearts
Bring your comfort to our fears.

When rhyme and reason disappears
As light of day into the night,
Stand by us Lord and lift us up!

Lift us up with gentle arms
Wipe away our futile tears
Heal our pain and mend our hearts
Bring your comfort to our fears.

When our failing faith is weak
Unlike your servant Job,
Stand by us Lord and lift us up!

Lift us up with gentle arms
Wipe away our futile tears
Heal our pain and mend our hearts
Bring your comfort to our fears.

When all the tears we've cried
Can't wash away the heartache,
Stand by us Lord and lift us up!

Lift us up with gentle arms
Wipe away our futile tears

13

Heal our pain and mend our hearts
Bring your comfort to our fears.

When at last we're on our knees
Where <u>first</u> we should have been,
Stand by us Lord and lift us up!

Lift us up with gentle arms
Wipe away our futile tears
Heal our pain and mend our hearts
Bring your comfort to our fears.

When we wait upon your mercy
And plead for better days,
Stand by us Lord and lift us up!

Lift us up with gentle arms
Wipe away our futile tears
Heal our pain and mend our hearts
Bring your comfort to our fears.

State of Grace

Our sins forgiven
We strive to follow Jesus
Yet daily we sin

Imperfect is man
Always seeking forgiveness
Already given

Danger!

Deception is contagious,
A wicked viral disease
That spreads from one
To another
Our very lives to seize.
A secret never stays secret
Of that you can be sure!
You can't even count
On your friends…
Their silence may not endure.
You can only count on yourself
To be totally honest and true
And ask yourself if God
Would be pleased
With what you're about to do!

*****

Each and every day
I sin in the eyes of God
Yet His grace forgives.

*****

Finally seeing
The radiance of Your face –
Heavenly reward

Heaven Bound

Do you know the way
To Heaven today?
It's no easy road
To carry your load
Up to the gates of
Heaven.

You can't get in
If you still have sin!
If you just commit one
Your chances are none
To enter the gates of
Heaven.

Repentance is key
For both you and me
And baptism too
Is required of you
To enter the gates of
Heaven.

Then salvation you'll earn
And when it's your turn
Get down on your knees
And thank God that you're free
To enter the gates of
Heaven

I Believe

Don't tell me that dogs don't go to Heaven or I might not want to go.
Have you been to Heaven and seen it? If not, how do you know?
If you say that animals have no souls, you've never looked into their eyes
And seen the very soul of God so cleverly disguised.
If heaven is supposed to be everything good we've ever dreamed,
The animals we've loved must be there or Heaven is not what it seems.
Faith is a very powerful tool. It can move mountains we are told.
"All things are possible to him who believes." That's how miracles unfold.
I have faith that I will see them again – all the pets that I have loved.
And if my faith is strong enough, I'll see them up above!

Mark 9:23
Mark 11:23-24
Matthew 9:29, 8:13, 19:26

My Father's Lap

When I was just a little child
I had a special place.
I would crawl into my father's lap
And kiss him on the face.
The love that I would find there
When hugged in his strong arms
Would comfort me and let me know
He'd keep me from all harm.
And now that I am growing old,
I look forward to going home
To see my heavenly Father
As He sits upon His throne.
He'll smile and motion me to come
Into His warm embrace
And on His lap I'll snuggle up
And kiss Him on His face.
A father's love is like that…
Comforting and true.
With arms forever open
To welcome me and you!

Trying to Be More Like God

Man was made in the image of God
Yet so much has changed since then.
The world is awash with evil and sin
And nothing today seems odd.

And yet there are some who try
To remember the words of the Lord
To meet together in one accord
And live right 'til His time is nigh.

Trying to walk as Jesus walked
On the straight and narrow way
Reading the Bible every day
And trying to talk the talk.

Allways reaching higher and higher
Trying to be more and more like God.
Signing on daily to the Master's squad
Working together with hearts afire.

Sweet Music

I have a song within my heart,
Silenced by the throes of life…
If only I could start
To hear the melody again
Like sparkling waters,
Crystal clear.

Sweet music hides within my soul.
While cymbalic clangs point out my fears,
Understanding can now unfold
And from guarded memories
New light appears.

There are no lyrics to my song,
No notes fill the empty page;
Just keening high and long,
Mournful arpeggios –
Pleas meant only for
The Master's ears.

Once Upon A Prayer

Once upon a prayer
I asked the Lord just where
I could find the answers.

"The answers to what my child?"

There's so many questions!
Would you have suggestions?
You know my heart's desire!

"Now wouldn't that be wild?"

Not wild to think you know my mind,
Not wild to ask you for a sign.
I can't figure it out on my own!

"Perhaps you need to pray harder."

That's just what I'm doing you see.
I thought your advice was free.
Who else can point the way?

"You need no other choice."

But I get discouraged, you know?
And I don't know where else to go
Except to you on my knees.

"When I'm ready, I'll give you my answer"

And then I finally knew the answer…
It was patience that He taught me
Once upon a prayer.

A New Year, A New You

Out with the old, in with the new
To clean up your soul, instructions are few:
Just believe in Jesus, God's only son
And know that together they become one;
Confess this belief and repent of your sins,
Be baptized/submerged while asking Him in.
Your life will be changed as will your heart
While the Spirit works wonders as he does his part.
But you too must contribute - you're not exempt,
For Satan will whisper and continue to tempt.
So fight back with vigor and keep spreading His Word
And His Light will shine forth as His message is heard!

I surrender all
Into God's hands and control
For He alone rules.

2

Rambling On About
Everyday Life

Holiday High

High atop
The Christmas tree
A star is shining bright
While garlands wrap
The boughs of green
Adorned with twinkling lights.
Ornaments old and new
Pulling families closer,
Remembering other nights
And other times together
Singing carols hand in hand
All in tune… not quite!
Traditions they will
All hold dear on future
Christmas nights!

Stranger than Fiction

Surely you must be mistaken!
What you propose cannot be true.
You saw eight reindeer up in the air
Pulling a sleigh all bright and new?!

The driver was old and rotund
With cheeks all red and aglow?
With a flowing white beard
And a booming "Ho, Ho, Ho!"?

Surely you must be mistaken!
I don't believe what you say…
The lead reindeer had a big red nose
That glowed to light their way?

And you saw bags of gifts in tow
Delivered from house to house
As he descended down chimneys
As quiet as any old mouse?

Surely you must be mistaken!
You try too hard to deceive
With your far-fetched Christmas story
That not even a child could believe!

Lunchtime Inspiration
(Florida Authors and Books Festival)

The order has been placed
The courier is on her way.
It won't be long before lunch is served
And we take a break to pray.
The crowd of "lookers" is waning.
There's a break in the conversation.
Time to consider a new poem
And enjoy the contemplation.
Sometimes the words will flow.
Sometimes they are elusive.
Sometimes the thoughts within
Are vague and inconclusive.
But we must take our inspiration
Whenever and wherever it comes
Whether it flows like a river or
        drops in like a rock
Leaving our senses raw and numb.

Weighted

Excitement?
I don't know how
To be excited.
I've tried before
But found the weight
Of it too much to bear.
Excitement
Brings disappointment
Following closely
In its footsteps.
It hangs like a brick
Around the neck
Of the doomed
Before he is tossed
Into the roiling sea.
Excitement
Has long since
Disappeared from
My emotional
Vocabulary.

Disappointment

Stalk and wait and pounce…
Watching the cat and the bird –
Too late! Empty paws!

*****

Teaching your dog by
Reward supplies hours of
Entertaining antics
And often questions who is
Training who!

*****

Alphabet
Soup –
Numberless meals

*****

Double Fudge Brownies

Baked and cut in squares
Dark and gooey chocolate –
Irresistible

Chocolate
Pie –
Sinfully good!

*****

When I Grow Up

When I grow up I want to be
A sassy old centenarian
With lots of boring life stories
To share again and again.

When I grow up I want to be
Able to laugh and to cry
At most inappropriate times
And keep people wondering why.

When I grow up I want to be
Sure that I've done things right
As the years disappeared…
No guilt to keep me up nights.

When I grow up I want to be
Healthy, wealthy and wise
And smart enough to thank God
For keeping me fit and alive!

Milestones Good and Bad

There are often events in our lives
Which effect our lives and others.
Milestones marking certain years
With love or terrible heartache.
Some we'd like to totally erase…
Others we try hard to remember.
It's the joy we want to hold onto,
Not the stupid, foolish mistakes.
But no matter how hard we try
Time itself will prove the key
As our years continue to climb,
Our memories may coil like a snake
As we wander through a gathering fog
And trip over precious memories
Which scurry away unseen
With each faltering step we take.
We must accept the good with the bad,
Each a building block weak or solid.
We must try to use them well for in life
There are very few remakes!

Hip Replacement Surgery

I've been dealing with this hip
For three long painful years.
Now it's time to get it replaced;
But I find nothing is ever easy.
So many tests need to be done
And the results must then be based
On the readings of the experts
In the field of cardiology
So their degrees don't go to waste!
But they take their own good time
And when you go to get pre-registered
You still must wait and wait
While they call and fax and read
And ponder if they'll get it done
Before it's way too late.
It's a long and frustrating process
But at last it's winding down
Just one more nurse to face.
So many instructions to remember!
I'm afraid my brain may slip a gear
Before that so important date!

Oscar Nomination (Please!)

Two more days and two nights
And I'm on my way
Departing for the bright lights…
Of the operating room.

It's my day to be a star!
Everyone's attention
On me…yes me!
It just can't come too soon!

Lying on the table,
Playing my roll,
I'll pose just right,
As I'm directed to do.

"Hey Doc, can I watch?"
I'll be tempted to ask,
But by that time I know
My options will be few.

I'll be departing into dreams
Of Academy awards
For my stellar performance
Once the anesthesia is applied.

And when I awake
With a brand new hip
I'll perform again with a smile
As the pain I try to hide.

It will take some time
To be as "good as new"
But I'll work real hard
To learn my new role.

For one day soon
I'll be striding on out …
Walking down that red carpet
To receive my Oscar of gold!

Medicine Today

Science and technology
Have come a long, long way.
Better drugs and treatments
Improving every day.
Robotic operating rooms,
New surgical methods and skills
Bring better, faster healing
But don't seem to lower the bills!

The Old Porch Swing

I can see it now
And hear the squeak
As back and forth
She pushed her feet.
Granny loved the old
Porch swing.

The children came
And climbed aboard
To get her hugs
As laughter roared
And love filled the old
Porch swing.

Yet now it hangs
In silence… alone
For Granny's passed
And the children, grown,
Have abandoned the old
Porch swing.

Dark

It's almost night now.
The sunset is fading fast.
Evening shadows grow.

Not Me

I've never been an authority
Or ever wanted to be.
I just muddle along
In the middle of the road
Trying to avoid the jostle
Of life passing by
Around me.

When you know enough
To be an authority
Everyone wants your advice.
You become the "go to" person
At everyone's beck and call
With no time of
Your own.

My Child

The moment I saw your face
I was lost.
All scrunched up and red…
And what a voice!
How can anyone love
In an instant
What caused them such pain …
We have no choice!
The moment I saw your face
My heart burst
With love and awe and joy
At your creation.
Mothers love. It's what we do,
As God intended.
We love, protect and teach.
It's our heavenly dispensation!

Across the Sea

Across the sea
Waves roll as winds churn the waters.
Across the sea
Dolphins frolic and play together.
Across the sea
Sunlight sparkles, dancing joyfully.
Across the sea
Thunder sends a warning far below.
Across the sea
A storm is brewing - Beware!

Looking Back

Looking back
I see I could have made
Better decisions,
Choices.

Life is strange,
Blinding you to reality
Deafening inner
Voices.

You see what
You want to see and ignore
The obvious
Problems

Until you're
Forced to face the truth and
Consequences
Of them.

On Being a Mother

Little did I know
The joy of motherhood
Until you appeared.

Little did I know
The pain of separation
Until you left home.

Little did I know
Old age until I saw you
Growing old also.

The Boiling Point

It takes a bit of heat to make me boil.
But when I reach that point
The unlucky soul who brought it on
Had better leave the joint!
Wild words may leave my lips,
Words I didn't want to say.
Boiling forth in hurtful wrath
Like demons in devilish play.
But eventually my anger is spent
And my pot begins to simmer.
The tears may flow and I may weep
As my waning anger grows dimmer.
Then just take me in your arms
And try to hold on tight
And tell me how much you love me
All through the tear-stained night.

Is It Time?

He's determined to die.
He keeps repeating it.
Won't let you forget
He wants to go.

Today is the day.
He seems so certain
But he could be wrong
For only God knows.

No Shelter

My thoughts are a jumble…
A desert of shifting sands
Dividing my mind into hills
And valleys of mismatched
Emotions and memories
Blowing this way and that
As my restless days are buffeted
By life's storms.

Waiting...

Swirls of blue
And dropping leaves
Spinning in circles
The earth receives
Light and shadows
Intermingled.

Quiet descends
Where once was shouting,
While those left behind
Seem to be pouting,
Unable to smile -
Frozen faces
Waiting, praying.

Bodiless voices
Instruct and chatter
While you sit and wait
For the one that matters
And the beat of a heart
Strengthened by science
And God's loving grace.

3

Rambling On About Quilting

A "Keeper"

Sometimes when I'm making a quilt
I put together a lovely design
And then find myself riddled with guilt
When the finishing gets out of line.
Stitches may pull or the fabric shift,
Or the borders stretch and get wavy.
I may just be careless, or my attention drift,
But I fall short of the perfection I crave.
There's no one to blame but me.
I can't rightly transfer the blame.
It's a "keeper" now don't you see? ...
Another utility quilt with no name.

My Passion, the Quilt

Somehow I never realized
The value of a quilt
Until I joined a guild
And my knowledge built
Block by block by block
As I learned the special skills
Needed to put one together
And my passion to fulfill.
When I was young I slept
Beneath my Granny's quilts
And now I long hold them
But must cry as "the milk is spilt"
And all her quilts are gone…
Tossed out or given away
By folks who knew not the value
Those quilts would have today.
So I just keep on sewing
Using patterns both old and new,
For my passion has not abated
And my love of quilting is true!

By Hand or Machine?

To quilt by hand or quilt by machine
Is always a question in quilt design.
Do you turn your work over to someone else
To mechanically finish your lovely creation
With swirls or stipples or creative new lines
Or do you want to quilt it yourself, by hand,
In traditional stitches or try something new
If it just didn't take so much of your time?
It's a question all quilters consider.
And the right answer is usually found
In the folds of the green in your wallet.
The cost of professional quilting today
Is not usually financially sound.
For those of us living from dollar to dollar
The fee per square inch is too high
When other choices abound.
To quilt by hand or quilt by machine
Is always a question in quilt design.
Of course there's always your home machine
Where you can learn to "do it yourself."
Amateurish would describe my wavering lines
When I try to "quilt as you go."
So for me I'll stick with hand quilting
Since that way turns out just fine!

Patchwork

I've often heard men wonder
Why a woman cuts up her cloth…
(Perfectly beautiful fabric,
Delightfully rich and soft)
Only to sew it together again
Into one quilt block or another,
Then build those blocks into a quilt
Like the one Granny made for Mother.
Men just don't understand it
They shake their heads, confused.
But don't they do the same
With the lumber that they choose
To cut and then nail together
Into art or a home's foundation
As they trudge through piles of sawdust
While basking in the joy of creation?
There's the answer folks right there –
The joy of creation is the thing…
A sense of personal accomplishment
And the satisfaction that it brings
When seeing the design you thought of,
Or the one you chose from a book,
Looking beautiful in your home
Or in someone's appreciative look.
It's the same with our patchwork of days,
Sewn together with love and sorrow,
As we try to pattern the life we live
Into a masterpiece others can borrow,

4

Rambling On About Death

(I have long been a fan of the country-western duo Joey and Rory. I have followed their progress and success ever since they appeared on the TV show "Can You Duet?"

It was with a joyous heart that I learned Joey was finally pregnant. And it was with a sad heart that I learned their new daughter, Indiana, was born with Downs Syndrome. When a little later Joey was diagnosed with cervical cancer, I prayed along with thousands of others for her successful treatment and recovery. And it was with a broken heart that I learned this aggressive cancer would take her life.

I have faithfully followed Rory's blog, "This Life I Live," and watched through his pictures and dialog as the family stood by her and encouraged her as they acknowledged and came to grips with the truth… God was going to take Joey home.

As Joey's days are winding down, my final poem is in her memory.)

Rory's Lament

The day after today,
The day after tomorrow,
The day after forever
Won't ease my sorrow.

When you went away
The sun stopped shining.
The clouds turned to gray
And there's no silver lining.

There are weeds in your garden
Where vegetables grew
And the sun doesn't sparkle
On the morning dew.

Across the wide field
Where the stones are marked
You lie with the others
In the damp and the dark.

The music is gone
The notes are adrift
On a page without lines
To anchor their shift

From country to gospel
To sweet lullaby.
As I cuddle our baby
My heart screams "Why?!"

But God had a plan
When he gave us each other
When he made you a star
And a sweet loving mother.

He shared you with me
And then with the world
And through you came Indy
Our sweet little girl.

Lord, we struggle to accept
That it is Your will
Please give us strength Lord
And our empty hearts fill.

Give us hope for an end
To our sadness and sorrow;
But it won't be today
Or the day after tomorrow.

www.ingramcontent.com/pod-product-compliance
Lightning Source LLC
Chambersburg PA
CBHW071738020426
42331CB00008B/2076